CW00496322

Liberty Phi

TAURUS

INTRODUCTION

Astrology is all about the planets in our skies and what energy and characteristics influence us. From ancient times, people have wanted to understand the rhythms of life and looked to the skies and their celestial bodies for inspiration, and the ancient constellations are there in the 12 zodiac signs we recognise from astrology. The Ancient Greeks devised narratives related to myths and legends about their celestial ancestors, to which they referred to make decisions and choices. Roman mythology did the same and over the years these ancient wisdoms became refined into today's modern astrology.

The configuration of the planets in the sky at the time and place of our birth is unique to each and every one of us, and what this means and how it plays out throughout our lives is both fascinating and informative. Just knowing which planet rules your sun sign is the beginning of an exploratory journey that can provide you with a useful tool for life.

Understanding the meaning, energetic nature and power of each planet, where this sits in your birth chart and what this might mean is all important information and linked to your date, place and time of birth, relevant only to you. Completely individual, the way in which you can work with the power of the planets comes from understanding their qualities and how this might influence the position in which they sit in your chart.

What knowledge of astrology can give you is the tools for working out how a planetary pattern might influence you, because of its relationship to your particular planetary configuration and circumstances. Each sun sign has a set of characteristics linked to its ruling planet – for example, Taurus is ruled by Venus – and, in turn, to each of the 12 Houses (see page 81) that form the structure of every individual's birth chart (see page 78). Once you know the meanings of these and how these relate to different areas of your life, you can begin to work out what might be relevant to you when, for example, you read in a magazine horoscope that there's a Full Moon in Capricorn or that Jupiter is transiting Mars.

Each of the 12 astrological or zodiac sun signs is ruled by a planet (see page 52) and looking at a planet's characteristics will give you an indication of the influences brought to bear on each sign. It's useful to have a general understanding of these influences, because your birth chart includes many of them, in different house or planetary configurations, which gives you information about how uniquely you you are. Also included in this book are the minor planets (see page 102), also relevant to the information your chart provides.

TAURUS

Our sun sign is determined by the date of our birth wherever we are born, and if you are a Taurus you were born between April 20th and May 20th. Bear in mind, however, that if you were born on one or other of those actual dates it's worth checking your time of birth, if you know it, against the year you were born and where. That's because no one is born 'on the cusp' (see page 78) and because there will be a moment on those days when Aries shifts to Taurus, and Taurus shifts to Gemini. It's well worth a check, especially if you've never felt quite convinced that the characteristics of your designated sun sign match your own.

The constellation of Taurus, the Latin word for bull, takes the shape of a bull's horns and charging front legs, with Aldebaran, the fourteenth brightest star in the sky, as the bull's eye. Taurus is forever associated with the god Zeus, king of the heavens, who disguised himself as a beautiful white bull in order to seduce Europa, the daughter of the king of Phoenicia.

Taurus is ruled by the Roman goddess Venus, so this sign embodies many of the qualities gifted by this planet, including a deep love and appreciation of beautiful things, and a gracious and elegant approach to life.

An earth sign (like Virgo and Capricorn), Taurus tends to be grounded in attitude, pragmatic about life and secure in themselves. It takes quite a lot to knock Taurus off course because they are also a fixed sign (like Leo, Scorpio and Aquarius) and show commitment, stamina and endurance, making them very good at seeing things through to completion, with the perseverance to stay the course and complete the job. Their creativity with problem-solving and other areas of life is strong, and evident through delivering on their ideas and ensuring the necessary work gets done. Never underestimate Taurus' ability to produce something beautiful as well as useful; what it looks like is as important as its function.

The sign ♉ of Taurus shows the head and horns of the bull and also a cup on top of a circle, representing a container for material possessions or wealth. The bull represents the grounded dynamism of this sign.

PHYSICAL POWER
Taurus rules the throat and consequently the voice, which can be particularly attractive but easily affected by emotion.

SACRED GEMSTONE
Emerald, Aventurine, Peridot and the rare Tsavorite Garnet. Each has its own intrinsic property that resonates with Taurean characteristics, but all embody honesty, growth and peace.

OPPOSITE SIGN
Scorpio

Taurus is depicted by the bull, and often interpreted as stubborn because they like to hold their ground, but this belies a nature that can be both fierce *and* gentle and it would be a mistake to underestimate the loving heart of a Taurus.

Also renowned for reliability, if given a brief and a deadline, there's a tenacity about Taurus that ensures the job is done and done well, even beautifully, as there's also a tendency to go the extra mile to make it so, even if it's the most mundane of tasks. Because of this tendency to go the extra mile, Taureans may need to take care that they aren't taken advantage of or have their good will exploited, because this is something that can, in the last resort, cause an eruption. The bull will only take so much and woe betide someone who pushes them too far; they don't always forget and forgive so easily, either.

Ruled by Venus, key to Taurus is a love of beauty that can be seen in the way Taurus lives, from the graceful way they move to what they wear and how they furnish their homes. They are not averse to accumulating wealth so that they can create a home full of lovely or valuable objects, and are prepared to work hard to achieve this. And with a keen eye for what's visually pleasing, Taurus often thrives in artistic environments or workplaces. They are also quite hands on, being literally and metaphorically unafraid of 'getting their hands dirty' to acquire what they need, in particular to feel secure. That's another Taurean trait: a need for security and a need for a base which they can call home, and whether it's a studio flat or a mansion they make it their own through decorating it beautifully.

There's an immediate powerful energy about Taurus that's captivating, but this is sometimes focused on what *they* want to do and they can be rather inflexible about it. If everyone's in agreement, that's great. If there's some dissent, however, Taurus should remember that some negotiation can be helpful. A fixed attitude is what gives rise to the notion that Taurus can be a bit stubborn. It's worth remembering that this is the moment for some of that famous charm, another key characteristic of those ruled by Venus, because, as the saying goes, you catch more flies with honey than vinegar.

This Venus-led, gracious and accommodating side of Taurus means others are likely to see you as a serene, capable and well-organised presence who is easily trusted for their sound advice and relied upon for their input. What's not always obvious is the more sensitive side to Taurus, someone who needs to feel secure; when they don't, it can bring out a more dogmatic aspect of their character, stubbornly standing their ground until they are reassured.

THE MOON IN
YOUR CHART

While your zodiac sign is your Sun sign, making you a sun sign Taurus, the Moon also plays a role in your birth chart and if you know the time and place of your birth, along with your birth date, you can get your birth chart done (see page 78). From this you can discover in which Zodiac sign your Moon is positioned in your chart.

The Moon reflects the characteristics of who you are at the time of your birth, your innate personality, how you express yourself and how you are seen by others. This is in contrast to our Sun sign, which indicates the more dominant characteristics we reveal as we travel through life. The Moon also represents the feminine in our natal chart (the Sun the masculine) and the sign in which our Moon falls can indicate how we express the feminine side of our personality. Looking at the two signs together in our charts immediately creates a balance.

MOON IN TAURUS

The Moon spends roughly 2.5 days in each zodiac sign as it moves through all 12 signs during its monthly cycle. This means that the Moon is regularly in Taurus, and it can be useful to know when this occurs and in particular when we have a New Moon or a Full Moon in Taurus because these are especially good times for you to focus your energy and intentions.

A New Moon is always the start of a new cycle, an opportunity to set new intentions for the coming month, and when this is in your own sign, Taurus, you can benefit from this additional energy and support. The Full Moon is an opportunity to reflect on the culmination of your earlier intentions.

NEW MOON
IN TAURUS AFFIRMATION

'I am at one with the Earth and feel its strength
beneath my feet even when I look up and into the
sky. I pay heed to the Earth and trust its ancient
rhythm and cycles to support me.'

FULL MOON
IN TAURUS AFFIRMATION

'I am born of the Earth and to the Earth will I return,
and in this knowledge I will cherish it and aspire to
do my best to care for it for future generations.'

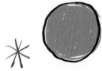

TAURUS
HEALTH

Taurus rules the throat and many have lovely speaking or singing voices, but it can also be an area of vulnerability. Not just a susceptibility to sore throats and laryngitis, but also to problems with the thyroid gland which is situated in the throat. A stiff neck, perhaps from long hours at the computer, is another point of tension, so learn some self-massage techniques (or ask a friend) to avoid that crick in the cerebral vertebrae.

Exercise is seldom very high on the Taurus agenda and they are not natural gym bunnies, or competitive enough as a team player, unless perhaps there's the promise of a massage afterwards. Because team sports aren't of particular interest, yoga or Pilates might appeal more, especially more grounded floor work, and especially if it can be gently incorporated into everyday life with a simple morning routine alongside a regular (or occasional) class. One simple way to factor in some daily exercise is to walk, and this will appeal to many Taureans because it keeps them in constant touch with the security of the ground beneath their feet. Taking the stairs rather than the elevator is another quick win to power up and strengthen those legs, while keeping hips and waist slim.

POWER UP
YOUR TAURUS
ENERGY

There are often moments or periods when we feel uninspired, demotivated and low in energy. At these times it's worth working with your innate sun sign energy to power up again, and paying attention to what Taurus relishes and needs can help support both physical and mental health.

Reconnect with the earthiness of your sign by taking a walk and grounding yourself in nature. Whatever the season, you can admire the sunlight, the wind, the leaves on the trees or the bare twigs against a winter sky. And it's important for Taurus to look up and lighten up when they feel down. As an earth sign it's all too easy to 'go to ground' when tired and depleted. While there's much to be gained from an occasional duvet day, and real rest is sometimes very necessary, remember to find ways to lift your spirits and lighten your soul.

Lighten your soul by looking at something you find beautiful; for example, enjoying a natural landscape or participating in its creation in some way by planting seeds, plants or bulbs. Visit a local art gallery or enjoy a music concert to refresh your soul. Getting out and about helps to avoid rumination, something the more bovine amongst us – and Taurus is naturally bovine – must remember.

Depression is often characterised by rumination and while Taurus isn't particularly given to mental health problems, we can all be susceptible when times are difficult.

Nurture your body too by cooking a delicious and nutritious meal and enjoying the process of preparing and sharing a meal with friends who appreciate you and whose company you enjoy. Make sure your comfort food is nutritious and supportive of Taurus energy and avoid overdosing on carbohydrates. Instead, choose foods that particularly chime to your sign: leafy green vegetables, including spinach, kale and cavolo nero, but also beets, onions and garlic, asparagus and squash. To support your thyroid, also include foods containing natural iodine like fish and seafood, seaweed, eggs and dairy.

In addition, because Taurus is an earth sign and has a tendency towards being sluggish, it's worth noting what spices might put renewed pep in your step. Perhaps a sprinkle of freshly ground black pepper or cayenne on your food, or freshly grated ginger tea with lemon and a little honey, which is also good for a congested throat.

Utilise a New Moon in Taurus with a ritual to set your intentions and power up: light a candle, use essential oil of rosemary to stimulate your mood and concentration (this oil blends well with calming chamomile and uplifting grapefruit), focus your thoughts on the change you wish to see and allow time to meditate on this. Place your gemstone (see page 13) in the moonlight. Write down your intentions and keep in a safe place. Meditate on the New Moon in Taurus affirmation (see page 21).

At a Full Moon in Taurus you will have the benefit of the Sun's reflected light to help illuminate what is working for you and what you can let go, because the Full Moon brings clarity. Focus on this with another ritual, taking the time to meditate on the Full Moon in Taurus affirmation (see page 21). Light a candle, place your gemstone in the moonlight and make a note of your thoughts and feelings, strengthened by the Moon in your sign.

TAURUS' SPIRITUAL HOME

Knowing where to go to replenish your soul and recharge your batteries both physically and spiritually is important and worth serious consideration. For some Taureans the kitchen is their spiritual home and many may also earn their living in the preparation of food, while others may find their voice in some way feeds their soul, singing for pleasure or profit.

Wherever they hail from, there are also a number of countries where Taurus will feel comfortable, whether they choose to go there to live, work or just take a holiday. These include the African country Tanzania, the Republic of Ireland, Switzerland and Australia, all of which resonate with grounded Taurean energy.

When it comes to holidays, Taurus often gravitates towards the more sensual pleasures of a natural habitat, whether this is walking or trekking through verdant pastures or woodlands, or seaside spa retreats with luxury treatments on tap. City breaks hold their appeal, especially for those Taureans that relish haute cuisine, whether eating or learning to cook it.

T A U

N

WOMAN

R U S

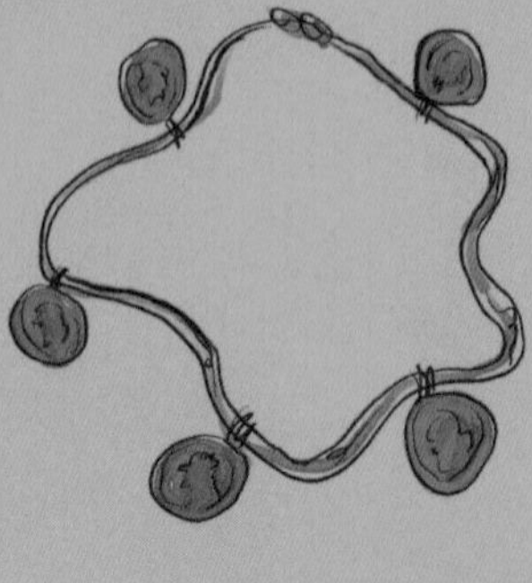

This is a woman who knows her own mind. Unsurprisingly, she is usually confident and secure in herself, something of an earth mother when it comes to taking care of herself and those around her, with a nurturing side that extends to cooking and often a keen appreciation of food. Not only might she enjoy cooking, she also enjoys creating a welcoming ambience and will take the time to make her dinner table look beautiful. This in turn is a reflection of her own need to seek or create a secure and beautiful environment, which she's happy to share with others.

Easy to spot, this is a woman who very much has her own distinctive look, with an eye for what suits her, and is usually of a very attractive appearance. Good at accessorising, she also likes good-quality materials and would prefer to buy a beautifully tailored vintage Chanel jacket than disposable fashion. Even if her physique is strong and athletic, even robust, there's still a gracefulness in her movement along with solidity and serenity, as Taurus is one of the more feminine of signs.

A natural confidante, she is a reliable keeper of secrets and non-judgemental about them too. She'll listen carefully to what is said, and her advice is often very practical and reassuring, her support consistent. If she says she will do something to help, you can believe it. That book she promised to lend you? She won't forget.

Inevitably straightforward in their approach, Taurean women are seldom afraid to show their true feelings, and this will include demonstrating their love and friendship, but also any displeasure. They are unlikely to sulk or go to sleep on a quarrel, preferring instead to clear the air, sort things out and sow the seeds of a fresh start immediately. When it comes to love, she won't commit until she's sure that her feelings are reciprocated. Unlikely to be sweet-talked by time-wasters, which she has an unerring ability to spot, this is a woman with an instinct for a reliable partner. If that sounds a bit dull, she needs to feel secure enough to reveal her playful side, so it's usually a win-win for both sides.

T A U

N

A

M

R U S

One of the first things you may notice about Taurus man is his appearance, not that he's flamboyant, but for the quality of his clothes: the linen of his shirt, the fine tweed of his jacket or his handmade leather brogues. He'd rather have a discreet wardrobe of well-chosen clothes than a casual look and if he can't yet afford top quality, he'll find it in vintage stores instead or opt for one or two key pieces rather than a wardrobe of throw-away excess.

He's the man that might even have his own tailor because ill-fitting clothes are not to his taste. Even his casual clothes speak of quality, and he is not averse to grooming products or even a manicure. This is a man who is likely to make the best of himself, not out of vanity but because he likes to feel secure and confident in his appearance and he truly appreciates the finer things in life.

This is also a man who knows how to stand his ground, and in social situations he's confident to sit alone and survey his surroundings rather than hide himself behind a book or trawling his phone. He won't mind if he's early for an appointment because he's happy to sit and ponder life, watching passers-by, comfortable with his own thoughts and in his own skin. His is a very definite, even powerful, presence and there's something reassuring and solid about it. Taurus man isn't particularly moody, but he is sometimes inclined to keep his own counsel until he's sure of where he stands.

With a practical bent and a kind heart, this is a man who probably knows how to put up a shelf and mend a fuse, and will offer to do so – even turning up with his own set of tools – but is also something of a romantic, prepared to put the effort into relationships of all kinds. He can be generous with time and money but is also sensitive to any rebuffs, so for all that seemingly resilient exterior, there's definitely a softer side.

TAURUS
IN LOVE

Ruled by Venus, Taurus is all about relationships, romance and even the art of romance. A first date is an occasion over which Taurus likes to take some time and trouble, whether it's a picnic in the park, a home-cooked meal or a night on the town. This is not a sign, however, that rushes into love but prefers to build relationships on something solid, perhaps a friendship that blossoms into a love affair. Taurus is patient in pursuit and will be content to play a long game once they've decided on the object of their affections, and they may well wait until the other person makes the first move too, in order not to risk rejection. Once committed, however, Taurus is a sensuous, generous and committed lover and not one to be fickle or take kindly to being treated in any way other than well. On that, they can be very stubborn because for Taurus, when it comes to love, they believe it should be reciprocated in kind.

TAURUS
AS A LOVER

There's a powerful sensuality to Taurus that can smoulder but is tempered sensitivity. No quickie before work; instead, the planet Venus ensures that there's a degree of finesse to their foreplay and this is likely to include wining and dining (to appeal to their epicurean nature), whether a kitchen supper or a five-star restaurant. In fact, Taurus may need some gentle encouragement to be more spontaneous, as their ardour is often couched in the security of a double bed rather than the hurly-burly of the chaise longue. What you will get is stamina. They are unlikely to use a headache as an excuse.

The art of seduction comes easily to Taurus but it is rooted in fidelity; this is not a sign given to rash declarations of love or one-night stands. They relish stability and as a consequence can be slow to make their move. However, because they also tend to trust their instincts, once they've focused on a potential lover they can be quite decisive, which can sometimes be alarming if it seems to come from nowhere. Taurus, don't crash into the china shop but give your new lover a bit of a clue that you're interested in getting to know them further.

Sex is often an extension of Taurus' innate physicality and sensuality. They have an appreciation of touch and foreplay is something to be savoured not rushed. In fact, many Taureans are into tantric sex, which is about connecting more deeply, focusing on sensation and connection. This is also where commitment comes in: sharing this intimacy with another rather than being profligate with their erotic side. But if this all sounds a bit intense, there's also an earthy if not to say bawdy and humorous side to Taurus lovemaking, which is another way of showing their physical enjoyment.

WHAT'S IN TAURUS' BEDSIDE CABINET?

Essential massage oil with a lovely earthy scent like bergamot

A state-of-the-art, luxury vibrator: self-pleasure is pleasure, right?

A copy of *Delta of Venus* by Anaïs Nin

WHICH SIGN
SUITS TAURUS?

In relationships with Taurus, the sun sign of the other person and the ruling planet of that sign can bring out the best, or sometimes the worst, in a lover. Knowing what might spark, smoulder or suffocate love is worth closer investigation, but always remember that sun sign astrology is only a starting point for any relationship.

TAURUS
AND ARIES

Venus and Mars are often considered a match made in the celestial skies, but the fiery spontaneity of Aries may need to consider the more grounded nature of Taurus and learn to take more time over love.

TAURUS
AND TAURUS

Venus and Venus may just be a little too similar, and possibly competitive with each other, for this to work – unless they are prepared to consciously work harmoniously together to avoid locking horns.

TAURUS
AND GEMINI

Ruled by Mercury, Gemini can often run rings around Venus with their airy attitude to life, but handled well this can bring lightness to Taurus and a little more grounding to Gemini, which can be wonderful for both.

TAURUS
AND CANCER

Venus is happy to bask in the reflected light of the lovely Moon that makes everything so beautiful, so this is often a very successful partnership that genuinely enhances the finer qualities of the bull and the crab.

TAURUS
AND LEO

Unsurprisingly, the Sun gives Leo the sense that they are the centre of the universe which can either amuse or irritate Venus-ruled Taurus, who believes love is the greater power. Using their charms, Taurus will often beguile their way to Leo's heart.

TAURUS
AND VIRGO

Ruled by Mercury, Virgo is also an earth sign so these two recognise what makes each other thrive, and if Taurus can avoid stubbornness and Virgo avoid perfectionism there's likely to be a very harmonious future ahead.

TAURUS
AND LIBRA

Both are ruled by Venus and appreciate each other's love for the finer things in life, and because Libra is all about balance and diplomacy, they can lighten some of Taurus' earthy attitude with a little air, which is beautifully positive.

TAURUS
AND SCORPIO

Pluto can be a tricky partner for Venus, and these are two fixed signs as well, but if they are both smart and perceptive enough to recognise each other's magical qualities, this can be a surprisingly exciting and enduring match.

TAURUS AND
SAGITTARIUS

Expansive Jupiter can mesmerise Venus, making Sagittarius' adventurous spirit very attractive to more home-bound Taurus. If they can each accept some of the basic differences between them, there can be a lasting attraction and committed bond.

TAURUS AND CAPRICORN

There's a nice balance here: Saturn can be a hard taskmaster, so Capricorn will welcome Venus' more gentle touch while Taurus loves stability. Together they can build a strong bond on which to create a harmonious love match.

TAURUS AND AQUARIUS

Innovative Uranus can shake Taurus up and in this way Aquarius can open up horizons previously unexplored by the bull, making their journey together one of unexpected pleasure, each bringing their positive energy to the other.

TAURUS AND PISCES

Neptune, Pisces' ruler, brings a mystical side to this equation. Pisces can open up Taurus' more spiritual side while they in turn gain much needed security, their differences creating unique possibilities that enhance them both.

TAURUS
AT WORK

Generally speaking, once they've found the right outlet for their talents, Taurus just loves to work and makes an excellent boss, work colleague or employee thanks to their enjoyment of getting the job done. If this capacity for diligence goes unrecognised, Taurus is likely to look elsewhere but, if valued, nothing will stop them doing their best job. A shrewd judge of character, Taurus will also patiently wait until the time is right for them and make their move.

Taurus' career motivation may be to ensure that they have the material security that ensures a comfortable life, but it can't be said that money is their main driver; often Taurus earns well as a by-product of the steady progress they can make up the career ladder or because of some artistic ability. For those Taurus with an entrepreneurial streak, they're prepared to put in the groundwork to ensure the success of the project to which they're committed, and this can often be the slow development of an intrinsically good idea or the improvement of an old one.

When it comes to professions, we often find carpenters and gardeners amongst those born under the sign of Taurus, often elevated to architecture and design, interiors or horticulture because of their Venus-driven love of beauty. You may also find others that work with their hands – physiotherapists, surgeons, massage or beauty therapists, hairdressers and cooks – are Taurus. Finance is another area where Taurus has an affinity, unsurprisingly since it rules the 2nd House of finance and material security (see page 82). It's not so much that they have a head for maths, but an understanding of how finance imparts value and how commodities can be traded.

Taurus may not be content to stay at entry level delivering their services, however, as they can easily take these professions and turn them into businesses in some way, ensuring that their first expertise underwrites their later success. Never underestimate Taurus when it comes to business success; slow and steady wins the race. And even if that's not for every Taurus, there are very few who don't make the grade in the world of work.

TAURUS
AT HOME

Because Taurus rules the 2nd astrological House associated with what you value, including what you own and material security, the home is often a place of great importance. Buying a home often tops the list of acquisitions for many Taurus, not least because they recognise the financial security that can come from owning property and they may sometimes own more than one.

But a home is very much more than a pile of bricks with a roof for Taurus. It's also their place of comfort, and their choice of decor is likely to reflect this, along with noticeable good taste in their choice of furniture. No high-tech burnished steel and concrete of an industrial-style modernist dwelling; there are likely to be sensually textured furnishings and artwork reflecting their Venus-led appreciation of beauty. Often the decor is in earthy shades, terra cotta or burnt sienna, deep greens or pale ash wood or oak. Whatever their choices, you get a real sense of the Taurus persona reflected in their nurturing homes.

And because one of Taurus' priorities is the sheer pleasure of cooking, eating and sharing food with their friends, their kitchen may reflect this. Large open-plan kitchens where friends and guests can gather over a Sunday lunch or summer buffet reflects the hospitable nature of the more gregarious Taurus. For others, the kitchen is their solace where they are just as happy to produce something delicious.

Many Taureans will also extend their home into a space in which they can literally connect with the earth. Whether this is a window box of herbs, a four-acre estate, an allotment, conservatory or urban yard, there's likely to be an area in which they will want to grow flowers for their beauty, or vegetables and fruit to eat.

FREE
THE SPIRIT

Understanding your own sun sign astrology is only part of the picture. It provides you with a template to examine and reflect on your own life's journey but also the context for this through your relationships with others, intimate or otherwise, and within the culture and environment in which you live.

Throughout time, the Sun and planets of our universe have kept to their paths and astrologers have used this ancient wisdom to understand the pattern of the universe. In this way, astrology is a tool to utilise these wisdoms, a way of helping make sense of the energies we experience as the planets shift in our skies.

'A physician without a knowledge of astrology has no right to call himself a physician,' said Hippocrates, the Greek physician born in 460 BC, who understood better than anyone how these psychic energies worked. As did Carl Jung, the 20th-century philosopher and psychoanalyst, because he said, 'Astrology represents the summation of all the psychological knowledge of antiquity.'

THE 10 PLANETS

SUN

RULES THE ASTROLOGICAL SIGN OF LEO

Although the Sun is officially a star, for the purpose of astrology it's considered a planet. It is also the centre of our universe and gives us both light and energy; our lives are dependent on it and it embodies our creative life force. As a life giver, the Sun is considered a masculine entity, the patriarch and ruler of the skies. Our sun sign is where we start our astrological journey whichever sign it falls in, and as long as we know which day of which month we were born, we have this primary knowledge.

MOON

We now know that the Moon is actually a natural satellite of the Earth (the third planet from the sun) rather than a planet but is considered such for the purposes of astrology. It's dependent on the Sun for its reflected light, and it is only through their celestial relationship that we can see it. In this way, the Moon in each of our birth charts depicts the feminine energy to balance the masculine sun's life force, the ying to its yang. It is not an impotent or subservient presence, particularly when you consider how it gives the world's oceans their tides, the relentless energy of the ebb and flow powering up the seas. The Moon's energy also helps illuminate our unconscious desires, helping to bring these to the service of our self-knowledge.

MERCURY

Mercury, messenger of the gods, has always been associated with speed and agility, whether in body or mind. Because of this, Mercury is considered to be the planet of quick wit and anything requiring verbal dexterity and the application of intelligence. Those with Mercury prominent in their chart love exchanging and debating ideas and telling stories (often with a tendency to embellish the truth of a situation), making them prominent in professions where these qualities are valuable.

Astronomically, Mercury is the closest planet to the sun and moves around a lot in our skies. What's also relevant is that several times a year Mercury appears to be retrograde (see page 99) which has the effect of slowing down or disrupting its influence.

VENUS

The goddess of beauty, love and pleasure. Venus is
the second planet from the sun and benefits from
this proximity, having received its positive vibes.
Depending on which astrological sign Venus falls in
your chart will influence how you relate to art and
culture and the opposite sex. The characteristics of
this sign will tell you all you need to know about
what you aspire to, where you seek and how you
experience pleasure, along with the types of lover you
attract. Again, partly depending on where it's placed,
Venus can sometimes increase self-indulgence which
can be a less positive aspect of a hedonistic life.

MARS

RULES THE ASTROLOGICAL SIGN OF ARIES

This big, powerful planet is fourth from the sun and exerts an energetic force, powering up the characteristics of the astrological sign in which it falls in your chart. This will tell you how you assert yourself, whether your anger flares or smoulders, what might stir your passion and how you express your sexual desires. Mars will show you what works best for you to turn ideas into action, the sort of energy you might need to see something through and how your independent spirit can be most effectively engaged.

JUPITER

Big, bountiful Jupiter is the largest planet in our solar
system and fifth from the sun. It heralds optimism,
generosity and general benevolence. Whichever sign
Jupiter falls in in your chart is where you will find
the characteristics for your particular experience of
luck, happiness and good fortune. Jupiter will show
you which areas to focus on to gain the most and
best from your life. Wherever Jupiter appears in your
chart it will bring a positive influence and when it's
prominent in our skies we all benefit.

SATURN

Saturn is considered akin to Old Father Time, with all the patience, realism and wisdom that archetype evokes. Sometimes called the taskmaster of the skies, its influence is all about how we handle responsibility and it requires that we graft and apply ourselves in order to learn life's lessons. The sixth planet from the sun, Saturn's 'return' (see page 100) to its place in an individual's birth chart occurs approximately every 28 years. How self-disciplined you are about overcoming opposition or adversity will be influenced by the characteristics of the sign in which this powerful planet falls in your chart.

URANUS

The seventh planet from the sun, Uranus is the planet of unpredictability, change and surprise, and whether you love or loathe the impact of Uranus will depend in part on which astrological sign it influences in your chart. How you respond to its influence is entirely up to the characteristics of the sign it occupies in your chart. Whether you see the change it heralds as a gift or a curse is up to you, but because it takes seven years to travel through a sign, its presence in a sign can influence a generation.

NEPTUNE

Neptune ruled the sea, and this planet is all about deep waters of mystery, imagination and secrets. It's also representative of our spiritual side so the characteristics of whichever astrological sign it occupies in your chart will influence how this plays out in your life. Neptune is the eighth planet from the sun and its influence can be subtle and mysterious. The astrological sign in which it falls in your chart will indicate how you realise your vision, dream and goals. The only precaution is if it falls in an equally watery sign, creating a potential difficulty in distinguishing between fantasy and reality.

PLUTO

RULES THE ASTROLOGICAL SIGN OF SCORPIO

Pluto is the furthest planet from the sun and exerts a regenerative energy that transforms but often requires destruction to erase what's come before in order to begin again. Its energy often lies dormant and then erupts, so the astrological sign in which it falls will have a bearing on how this might play out in your chart. Transformation can be very positive but also very painful. When Pluto's influence is strong, change occurs and how you react or respond to this will be very individual. Don't fear it, but reflect on how to use its energy to your benefit.

YOUR SUN SIGN

Your sun or zodiac sign is the one in which you were born, determined by the date of your birth. Your sun sign is ruled by a specific planet. For example, Taurus is ruled by Venus but Gemini by Mercury, so we already have the first piece of information and the first piece of our individual jigsaw puzzle.

The next piece of the jigsaw is understanding that the energy of a particular planet in your birth chart (see page 78) plays out via the characteristics of the astrological sign in which it's positioned, and this is hugely valuable in understanding some of the patterns of your life. You may have your Sun in Taurus, and a good insight into the characteristics of this sign, but what if you have Neptune in Leo? Or Venus in Aries? Uranus in Virgo? Understanding the impact of these influences can help you reflect on the way you react or respond and the choices you can make, helping to ensure more positive outcomes.

If, for example, with Uranus in Taurus you are resistant to change, remind yourself that change is inevitable and can be positive, allowing you to work with it rather than against its influence. If you have Neptune in Virgo, it will bring a more spiritual element to this practical earth sign, while Mercury in Aquarius will enhance the predictive element of your analysis and judgement. The scope and range and useful aspect of having this knowledge is just the beginning of how you can utilise astrology to live your best life.

PLANETS IN TRANSIT

In addition, the planets do not stay still. They are said to transit (move) through the course of an astrological year. Those closest to us, like Mercury, transit quite regularly (every 88 days), while those further away, like Pluto, take much longer, in this case 248 years to come full circle. So the effects of each planet can vary depending on their position and this is why we hear astrologers talk about someone's Saturn return (see page 100), Mercury retrograde (see page 99) or about Capricorn (or other sun sign) 'weather'. This is indicative of an influence that can be anticipated and worked with and is both universal and personal. The shifting positions of the planets bring an influence to bear on each of us, linked to the position of our own planetary influences and how these have a bearing on each other. If you understand the nature of these planetary influences you can begin to work with, rather than against, them and this information can be very much to your benefit.

First, though, you need to take a look at the component parts of astrology, the pieces of your personal jigsaw, then you'll have the information you need to make sense of how your sun sign might be affected during the changing patterns of the planets.

YOUR BIRTH CHART

With the date, time and place of birth, you can easily find out where your (or anyone else's) planets are positioned from an online astrological chart programme (see page 110). This will give you an exact sun sign position, which you probably already know, but it can also be useful if you think you were born 'on the cusp' because it will give you an exact indication of what sign you were born in. In addition, this natal chart will tell you your Ascendant sign, which sign your Moon is in, along with the other planets specific to your personal and completely individual chart and the Houses (see page 81) in which the astrological signs are positioned.

A birth chart is divided into 12 sections, representing each of the 12 Houses (see pages 82–85) with your Ascendant or Rising sign always positioned in the 1st House, and the other 11 Houses running counter-clockwise from 1 to 12.

  ♉ TAURUS

ASCENDANT OR RISING SIGN

Your Ascendant is a first, important part of the complexity of an individual birth chart. While your sun sign gives you an indication of the personality you will inhabit through the course of your life, it is your Ascendant or Rising sign – which is the sign rising at the break of dawn on the Eastern horizon at the time and on the date of your birth – that often gives a truer indication of how you will project your personality and consequently how the world sees you. So even though you were born a sun sign Taurus, whatever sign your Ascendant is in, for example Cancer, will be read through the characteristics of this astrological sign.

Your Ascendant is always in your 1st House, which is the House of the Self (see page 82) and the other houses always follow the same consecutive astrological order. So if, for example, your Ascendant is Leo, then your second house is in Virgo, your third house in Libra, and so on. Each House has its own characteristics but how these will play out in your individual chart will be influenced by the sign positioned in it.

Opposite your Ascendant is your Descendant sign, positioned in the 7th House (see page 84) and this shows what you look for in a partnership, your complementary 'other half' as it were. There's always something intriguing about what the Descendant can help us to understand, and it's worth knowing yours and being on the lookout for it when considering a long-term marital or business partnership.

THE 12 HOUSES

While each of the 12 Houses represent different aspects of our lives, they are also ruled by one of the 12 astrological signs, giving each house its specific characteristics. When we discover, for example, that we have Capricorn in the 12th House, this might suggest a pragmatic or practical approach to spirituality. Or, if you had Gemini in your 6th House, this might suggest a rather airy approach to organisation.

1ST HOUSE

RULED BY ARIES

The first impression you give walking into a room, how you like to be seen, your sense of self and the energy with which you approach life.

2ND HOUSE

RULED BY TAURUS

What you value, including what you own that provides your material security; your self-value and work ethic, how you earn your income.

3RD HOUSE

RULED BY GEMINI

How you communicate through words, deeds and gestures; also how you learn and function in a group, including within your own family.

4TH HOUSE

RULED BY CANCER

This is about your home, your security
and how you take care of yourself and
your family; and also about those family
traditions you hold dear.

5TH HOUSE

RULED BY LEO

Creativity in all its forms, including fun
and eroticism, intimate relationships and
procreation, self-expression
and positive fulfilment.

6TH HOUSE

RULED BY VIRGO

How you organise your daily routine, your
health, your business affairs, and how you
are of service to others, from those
in your family to the workplace.

7TH HOUSE

RULED BY LIBRA

This is about partnerships and shared
goals, whether marital or in business,
and what we look for in these to
complement ourselves.

8TH HOUSE

RULED BY SCORPIO

Regeneration, through death and rebirth,
and also our legacy and how this might be
realised through sex, procreation
and progeny.

9TH HOUSE

RULED BY SAGITTARIUS

Our world view, cultures outside our
own and the bigger picture beyond our
immediate horizon, to which we travel
either in body or mind.

10TH HOUSE

RULED BY CAPRICORN

Our aims and ambitions in life, what we aspire
to and what we're prepared to do to achieve it;
this is how we approach our
working lives.

11TH HOUSE

RULED BY AQUARIUS

The house of humanity and our
friendships, our relationships with the
wider world, our tribe or group to which
we feel an affiliation.

12TH HOUSE

RULED BY PISCES

Our spiritual side resides here. Whether this is
religious or not, it embodies our inner
life, beliefs and the deeper connections
we forge.

THE FOUR
ELEMENTS

The 12 astrological signs are divided into four groups, representing the four elements: fire, water, earth and air. This gives each of the three signs in each group additional characteristics.

FIRE

ARIES ❧ LEO ❧ SAGITTARIUS

Embodying warmth, spontaneity and enthusiasm.

WATER

CANCER ❧ SCORPIO ❧ PISCES

Embody a more feeling, spiritual and intuitive side.

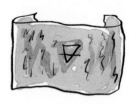

EARTH

TAURUS ≈ VIRGO ≈ CAPRICORN

Grounded and sure-footed and sometimes rather stubborn.

AIR

GEMINI ❧ LIBRA ❧ AQUARIUS

Flourishing in the world of vision, ideas and perception.

FIXED, CARDINAL OR MUTABLE?

The 12 signs are further divided into three groups of four, giving additional characteristics of being fixed, cardinal or mutable. These represent the way in which they respond to situations.

FIXED

TAURUS, LEO, SCORPIO AND AQUARIUS ARE FIXED SIGNS

Their energy tends to be steady and they are less reactive, more responsive, although they can have a tendency to be resistant to change and need encouragement.

CARDINAL

ARIES, CANCER, LIBRA AND CAPRICORN ARE CARDINAL SIGNS

Their energy is often instinctive and action-oriented, enabling them to get things started, although there's sometimes a tendency to fail to carry things through.

MUTABLE

GEMINI, VIRGO, SAGITTARIUS AND PISCES ARE MUTABLE SIGNS

The clue here is their adaptability and responsiveness to change, which they don't fear, and readiness to listen to and embrace new ideas.

MERCURY RETROGRADE

This occurs several times over the astrological year and lasts for around four weeks, with a shadow week either side (a quick Google search will tell you the forthcoming dates). It's important what sign Mercury is in while it's retrograde, because its impact will be affected by the characteristics of that sign. For example, if Mercury is retrograde in Gemini, the sign of communication that is ruled by Mercury, the effect will be keenly felt in all areas of communication. However, if Mercury is retrograde in Aquarius, which rules the house of friendships and relationships, this may keenly affect our communication with large groups, or if in Sagittarius, which rules the house of travel, it could affect travel itineraries and encourage us to check our documents carefully.

Mercury retrograde can also be seen as an opportunity to pause, review or reconsider ideas and plans, to regroup, recalibrate and recuperate, and generally to take stock of where we are and how we might proceed. In our fast-paced 24/7 lives, Mercury retrograde can often be a useful opportunity to slow down and allow ourselves space to restore some necessary equilibrium.

SATURN RETURN

When the planet Saturn returns to the place in your chart that it occupied at the time of your birth, it has an impact. This occurs roughly every 28 years, so we can see immediately that it correlates with ages that we consider representative of different life stages and when we might anticipate change or adjustment to a different era. At 28 we can be considered at full adult maturity, probably established in our careers and relationships, maybe with children; at 56 we have reached middle age and are possibly at another of life's crossroads; and at 84, we might be considered at the full height of our wisdom, our lives almost complete. If you know the time and place of your birth date, an online Saturn return calculator can give you the exact timing.

It will also be useful to identify in which astrological sign Saturn falls in your chart, which will help you reflect on its influence, as both influences can be very illuminating about how you will experience and manage the impact of its return. Often the time leading up to a personal Saturn return is a demanding one, but the lessons learnt help inform the decisions made about how to progress your own goals. Don't fear this period, but work with its influence: knowledge is power and Saturn has a powerful energy you can harness should you choose.

THE MINOR PLANETS

Sun sign astrology seldom makes mention of these 'minor' planets that also orbit the sun, but increasingly their subtle influence is being referenced. If you have had your birth chart done (if you know your birth time and place you can do this online) you will have access to this additional information.

Like the 10 main planets on the previous pages, these 18 minor entities will also be positioned in an astrological sign, bringing their energy to bear on these characteristics. You may, for example, have Fortuna in Leo, or Diana in Sagittarius. Look to these for their subtle influences on your birth chart and life via the sign they inhabit, all of which will serve to animate and resonate further the information you can reference on your own personal journey.

AESCULAPIA

Jupiter's grandson and a powerful
healer, Aesculapia was taught by
Chiron and influences us in what
could be life-saving action, realised
through the characteristics of the sign
in which it falls in our chart.

BACCHUS

Jupiter's son, Bacchus is similarly
benevolent but can sometimes lack
restraint in the pursuit of pleasure.
How this plays out in your chart is
dependent on the sign in which
it falls.

APOLLO

Jupiter's son, gifted in art, music and
healing, Apollo rides the Sun across
the skies. His energy literally lights up
the way in which you inspire others,
characterised by the sign in which it
falls in your chart.

CERES

Goddess of agriculture and mother of
Proserpina, Ceres is associated with
the seasons and how we manage cycles
of change in our lives. This energy is
influenced by the sign in which it falls
in our chart.

CHIRON

Teacher of the gods, Chiron knew all about healing herbs and medical practices and he lends his energy to how we tackle the impossible or the unthinkable, that which seems difficult to do.

DIANA

Jupiter's independent daughter was allowed to run free without the shackles of marriage. Where this falls in your birth chart will indicate what you are not prepared to sacrifice in order to conform.

CUPID

Son of Venus. The sign into which Cupid falls will influence how you inspire love and desire in others, not always appropriately and sometimes illogically but it can still be an enduring passion.

FORTUNA

Jupiter's daughter, who is always shown blindfolded, influences your fated role in other people's lives, how you show up for them without really understanding why, and at the right time.

HYGEIA

Daughter of Aesculapia and also associated with health, Hygeia is about how you anticipate risk and the avoidance of unwanted outcomes. The way you do this is characterised by the sign in which Hygeia falls.

MINERVA

Another of Jupiter's daughters, depicted by an owl, will show you via the energy given to a particular astrological sign in your chart how you show up at your most intelligent and smart. How you operate intellectually.

JUNO

Juno was the wife of Jupiter and her position in your chart will indicate where you will make a commitment in order to feel safe and secure. It's where you might seek protection in order to flourish.

OPS

The wife of Saturn, Ops saved the life of her son Jupiter by giving her husband a stone to eat instead of him. Her energy in our chart enables us to find positive solutions to life's demands and dilemmas.

PANACEA

Gifted with healing powers, Panacea
provides us with a remedy for all ills
and difficulties, and how this plays
out in your life will depend on the
characteristics of the astrological sign
in which her energy falls.

PSYCHE

Psyche, Venus' daughter-in-law, shows
us that part of ourselves that is easy to
love and endures through adversity,
and your soul that survives death and
flies free, like the butterfly that
depicts her.

PROSERPINA

Daughter of Ceres, abducted by Pluto,
Proserpina has to spend her life divided
between earth and the underworld and
she represents how we bridge the gulf
between different and difficult aspects
of our lives.

SALACIA

Neptune's wife, Salacia stands on
the seashore bridging land and sea,
happily bridging the two realities.
In your chart, she shows how you
can harmoniously bring two sides of
yourself together.

VESTA

Daughter of Saturn, Vesta's job was to protect Rome and in turn she was protected by vestal virgins. Her energy influences how we manage our relationships with competitive females and male authority figures.

VULCAN

Vulcan was a blacksmith who knew how to control fire and fashion metal into shape, and through the sign in which it falls in your chart will show you how you control your passion and make it work for you.

FURTHER READING

Jung's Studies in Astrology: Prophecies, Magic and the Qualities of Time,

Liz Greene, Routledge (2018)

Lunar Oracle: Harness the Power of the Moon,

Liberty Phi, OH Editions (2021)

Metaphysics of Astrology: Why Astrology Works,

Ivan Antic, Independently published (2020)

Parkers' Astrology: The Definitive Guide to Using Astrology in Every Aspect

of Your Life,

Julia and Derek Parker, Dorling Kindersley (2020)

USEFUL WEBSITES

Alicebellastrology.com

Astro.com

Astrology.com

Cafeastrology.com

Costarastrology.com

Jessicaadams.com

USEFUL APPS

Astro Future

Co-Star

Moon

Sanctuary

Time Nomad

Time Passages

ACKNOWLEDGEMENTS

Thanks are due to my Taurean publisher Kate Pollard for commissioning this Astrology Oracle series, to Piscean Matt Tomlinson for his careful editing, and to Evi O Studio for their beautiful design and illustrations.

ABOUT THE AUTHOR

As a sun sign Aquarius Liberty Phi loves to explore the world and has lived on three different continents, currently residing in North America. Their Gemini moon inspires them to communicate their love of astrology and other esoteric practices while Leo rising helps energise them. Their first publication, also released by OH Editions, is a box set of 36 oracle cards and accompanying guide, entitled *Lunar Oracle: Harness the Power of the Moon.*

Published in 2023 by OH Editions,
an imprint of Welbeck Non-Fiction Ltd,
part of the Welbeck Publishing Group.
Offices in London, 20 Mortimer Street, London, W1T 3JW,
and Sydney, 205 Commonwealth Street, Surry Hills, 2010.
www.welbeckpublishing.com

Design © 2023 OH Editions
Text © 2023 Liberty Phi
Illustrations © 2023 Evi O. Studio

A CIP catalogue record for this book is available from the British Library.

ISBN 978-1-91431-794-1

Publisher: Kate Pollard
Editor: Sophie Elletson
In-house editor: Matt Tomlinson
Designer: Evi O. Studio
Illustrator: Evi O. Studio
Production controller: Jess Brisley
Printed and bound by Leo Paper

MIX
Paper | Supporting
responsible forestry
FSC® C020056
www.fsc.org

10 9 8 7 6 5 4 3 2 1